Consumers
A letter from the Author

Hello,

Welcome to **Consumers**! We have lots of articles about different aspects of our modern world. Who are the consumers? What do they consume? Are there better ways of having a happy life in our consumer societies?

There are a lot of different facts, opinions, ideas and pictures in this Topics title. We're sure you'll find them interesting. We look at the shopping experience, at fashion and at advertising. There are articles about the environment, and making the world a better place to live in. And others about ways to improve our personal lives.

One more thing! Reading the articles is only the first stage. What about **your** ideas, opinions and experience? **Your** facts and photos? The Consumer Spy note suggests ideas for comparing your personal experience with the articles in these pages. Remember that the Projects page has ideas for extending them. So reading is just the beginning.

We really hope that you enjoy exploring these ideas.

Susan Holden

contents

- 2 Check it out
- 3 Let's go shopping!
- 4 Fashion: what's new?
- 6 Ad speak
- 8 Innovation, innovation, innovation!
- 10 Charity shops
- 11 The travels of a blouse
- 12 UNICEF works!
- 14 Phones can do anything!
- 15 The state of our planet
- 16 An environmental project
- 18 Consumer hot topics: obesity
- 20 Healthy living
- 21 Problem solving
- 22 Do you know?
- 23 Projects
- 24 Topics chatrooms

TO THE TOPICS USERS

VOCABULARY You can find the key vocabulary for every article in the **WORD FILE** on that page. The pictures will also help you guess the meaning in context. There is a summary of useful vocabulary on the **Check it out** page. Finally, you can use the *Macmillan English Dictionary* to consolidate the new vocabulary.

WEBSITES There is a list of useful website addresses on page 2. Remember that websites change. Be selective!

Check it out

Buying and selling

advertise	bargain	buy
export	import	market
package	pay	promote
sell	sponsor	swap
target	trade	window-shop

Nouns

Things

bargain	deal	product

Places

boutique	e-commerce	Internet
mall	market	retailer
shop 🇬🇧	store 🇺🇸	supermarket

People

advertiser	clerk 🇺🇸	client
customer	employee	employer
manufacturer	seller	shop assistant 🇬🇧

Adjectives

cheap	expensive	fashionable
'in'	memorable	persuasive

Money

Nouns

allowance 🇺🇸	bills 🇺🇸	cash
change	coins	credit card
currency	notes 🇬🇧	pocket money 🇬🇧

Resources
The environment

Verbs

destroy	exhaust	pollute
preserve	recycle	rescue
respect	reuse	save

Nouns

energy	environment	factory
farming	fuel	garbage 🇺🇸
industry	oil	resources
rubbish 🇬🇧	trash 🇺🇸	waste

Adjectives

ecological	ethical	inorganic
organic	processed	sustainable

Living

Verbs

breathe	diet	drink
eat	exercise	starve

Adjectives

anorexic	bored	bulimic
depressed	happy	hungry
obese	stressed	worried

Sources and Resources

We consulted a lot of sources for 'Consumers': people, books and the Internet. If you want to find out more about any of the topics, here are some useful Internet sites. Add your own favourite sites and other useful resources.

www.bbc.co.uk/cbbc
www.eco-schools.org.uk
www.foodstandards.gov.uk/healthiereating
www.fairtrade.org
www.wwf.org
www.unicef.org
www.trendsetters.org

LET'S GO SHOPPING!

Different people like to shop in different places. It all depends on you.

Something special for that special date?
Go to your favourite specialist fashion shop. Great clothes, great ideas... but they can be expensive.

Money a problem? Want a bargain, something really cheap?
Then maybe a street-market is best for you.

A lot of variety? No time to visit lots of different places?
Just go down to the supermarket.

Perhaps you just want a chance to look at the newest fashions. Why not go window-shopping? This is the cheapest way to shop!

But if you want *all* of these – ideas, variety, space, and special shops – then the shopping mall is the place for you. And, of course, it's also a place to hang out with your friends, to chat, and to make plans. Did you know that some of the newest malls in the U.S. and Canada now have special lounges for teenagers? There's a lot of life in a mall!

WORD FILE

bargain	Something that is good value for money.
chat (v)	To talk to your friends.
cheap	Does not cost much money.
expensive	Costs a lot of money.
go window-shopping (v)	To look in shop windows without buying anything.
hang out (v)	To be with your friends.
lounge	A room to sit, watch videos, read magazines and chat.
variety	A lot of different types of things.

🇺🇸 favorite store	🇬🇧 favourite shop

CONSUMER SPY — Do a survey on favourite shopping places. Where do you normally go? Where do your friends go? What are the percentages for different places? Do people's choices depend on age, personality or...?

Fashion: What's NEW?

Fashion involves change. Change involves finding new things. Finding new things involves buying, selling and making a profit. So… is fashion a good thing? It's fun, anyway. It feels good to wear something really new, to be really 'in'. But wait a minute! Is fashion always really new? Take a look at these fashion hits, past and present.

Mini-skirt

Pointed shoes

Flares

Ponytails

Cut

And then there's the fashion for 'old' things. Like a pair of jeans with holes. Fashion? Well, they're very expensive holes! But even holes in our clothes aren't modern. In the 15th and 16th centuries, rich people cut them to show the different colours under the surface.

WORD FILE
feel good (v)	To feel relaxed.
hit	Something that is very good and in fashion.
to be 'in' (v)	To be in fashion.

🇺🇸 color 🇬🇧 colour

So what's new?!

"Modern life is fast"

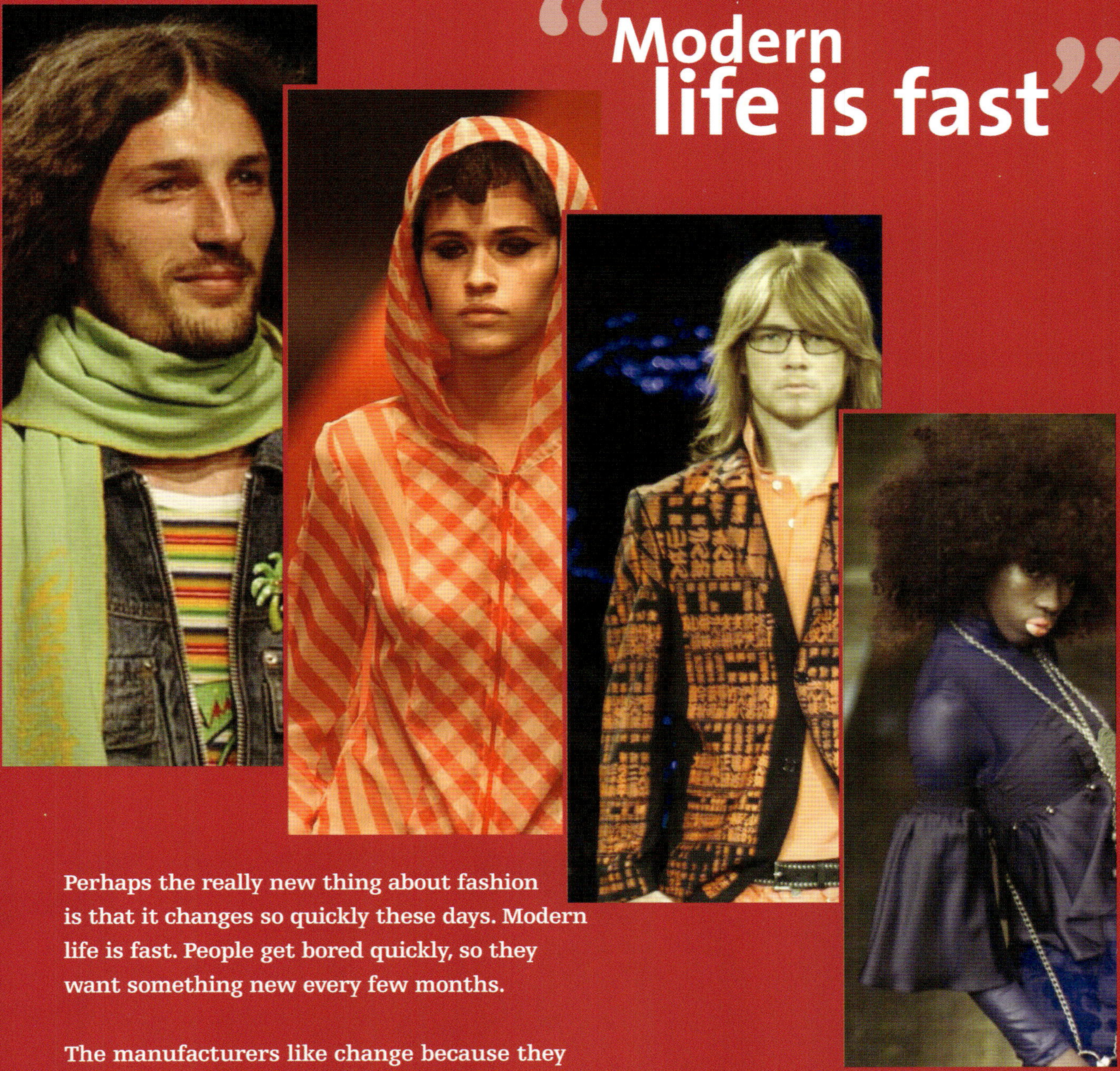

Perhaps the really new thing about fashion is that it changes so quickly these days. Modern life is fast. People get bored quickly, so they want something new every few months.

The manufacturers like change because they can sell new things. Ads encourage this appetite for change. (See the article on Ad Speak on page 6.)

What do people do with all their old things? Well, they throw a lot of them away. These old things often become rubbish. And what happens to this rubbish? See pages 12 and 13.

But not all old things are rubbish. Some of them are recycled. People make new things out of them. For example, it's possible to make paper out of old clothes. Other things are sold. The money is then used by charities to help other people. Read more about this on pages 10 and 11.

WORD FILE	
ad	Advertisement.
bored	With no interest in something.
charity	An organisation that helps poor or ill people.
encourage (v)	To inspire or support a person to do something.
garbage	Things you want to throw away.
manufacturer	A person or company that makes things.
recycle (v)	To reuse in a new way.
throw away (v)	To discard, give away.

🇺🇸 garbage   🇬🇧 rubbish
   sick   ill

Look at the clothes and personal possessions in your room. Try to remember *why* you bought them? Fashion? Did you need them? Did your friend have one? What is the strongest influence on you? Can you remember the date when you bought them. Choose five items.

CONSUMER SPY

5

Ad Speak

Advertising is all around us. It's on T.V., in magazines, in newspapers, on websites. It's difficult to escape it. Ads tell us about the product, right? Yes – but they do this in lots of different ways. They use images, words, sounds and word association.

Let's do a bit of ad analysis. We can find out what kind of message the advertisers are using. Are they trying to manipulate us? Or are they just giving us information?

For a start, ads can be INTRIGUING, PERSUASIVE, CHALLENGING…

WORD FILE

advertising	The activity of making and using ads.
challenging	Difficult, but interesting also.
hot fashion	Very new types of fashion items.
intriguing	Mysterious and strange.
manipulate (v)	To make somebody do something.
memorable	Easy to remember.
persuasive	Something that moves you through argument.
soft	Gentle.
subtle	Not obvious, difficult to notice.
whisper (v)	To speak very quietly.
word association	One word makes you think of another one.

INTRIGUING ADS

These often use beautiful – or strange – photos. They are designed to catch our attention, and to be memorable. The most extreme ads of this type do not even give the name of the object! They want to make us stop and look at them in a subtle way.
This type of ad is often used for cigarettes. Cigarette advertising is controlled in many countries, so advertisers try to find 'soft' ways to sell their product.

PERSUASIVE ADS

This type often uses 'gentle' messages. They 'suggest' something. It's like having your best friend whispering in your ear and smiling at you. "Why don't you…?", "Have you ever considered…?".

CHALLENGING ADS

"Be one of the group!" "All the coolest kids use this product!" "Why be different?" These ads often use aggressive language and images. They generally promote 'hot fashion' items – things that will go out of fashion very quickly!

To look great...
it's indispensable!

KONIA
Connected with the world

Do you agree with these groups of ads? Can you think of others? Find your own ads to illustrate each group. Which ones are the most effective?

WORD FILE	
benefit (v)	To get an advantage from something.
charity	An organisation that helps poor or sick people.
effectively	In an efficient way.
fool (v)	To make people believe something that isn't true.
funky	Fashionable in an unusual way.
hip	Modern and fashionable.
image-conscious	Conscious of your appearance.
shock (v)	To cause a big surprise.
smart	Not stupid.
starve (v)	To be without food.

🇺🇸	🇬🇧
cellphone	mobile
color	colour
sick	ill
smart	clever

IMAGE, IMAGE, IMAGE...

"Here's the coolest... wildest... hippest... funkiest... object!"
"The image-conscious person cannot do without it!"
This style is ideal for fashion and consumer objects (mobiles, backpacks, watches, and so on). It's the most common form of advertising for many products. But don't forget all those other types of message. Be clever: don't let the advertisers fool you!

SCIENTIFIC ADS

These ads often contain a lot of text. There's a 'scientific' explanation to support the product. Often there are letters from 'real people' who have benefitted from the product. Sometimes these ads use diagrams and statistics to give them an image of truth. You can find these ads for products like healthy food and drinks, medicine – and even health clubs.

SOCIAL CONSCIENCE ADS

Some advertising is designed to shock us. Sometimes the advertisers want to make us feel sorry for people who are less fortunate than us. They use images like starving kids, or people sleeping in the street. These remind us of the negative side of the consumer world. The photos are often in black and white. They appeal to our hearts and our consciences. Their message is "Give money". Charities use this type of advertising very effectively.

SHOCK! HORROR!

These ads are not *selling* anything. They want to STOP you from doing something. Think of problems like AIDS, smoking, drugs, alcohol. They use shocking visual images, strong colours and often statistics to shock us.

Innovation,

In every country, clever people are thinking of new ideas, new products – and new ways of selling them. Some of these ideas will disappear; others will be a great success. And some of them will make a lot of money.

What do you think of these new ideas? Will they be here in five years' time? Or will they be dead?

Mobile soaps!

Soaps are popular in many countries. Most T.V. channels show them. Soap fans always try to stay home to see the latest episode.

However, in the Netherlands, soap fans don't need to stay home to keep up to date! They can now register for a special soap opera on their mobiles. They register online, and receive two episodes a day. Each episode contains six video scenes with text. This new soap is about a group of young people who live together. There's lots of fun, drama and personal emotions.

There's a plus feature, too: if they win a competition, the viewers can take part in the soap.

What about money? Well, the subscribers pay US$1.20 a week. But soaps are very expensive to make. In fact, the characters in the drama wear fashionable clothes, and use new accessories. Big companies pay to have their products used in the soap. That's where the *big* money comes from!

And, of course, the soap company also keeps the personal details of the consumers' mobiles. So they can send them messages about new products. Everybody is happy!

WORD FILE

ethical	Follows ideas of what is morally right.
fan	A person who supports a film, a singer or a team.
plus feature	Something extra.
register (v)	To give your name and address to a company.
up to date	Very modern.
soap	Short for 'soap opera'.

🇺🇸 cellphone   🇬🇧 mobile

CONSUMER SPY — What do you think? Is this advertising? Is it innocent entertainment? Is it ethical?

Innovation, Innovation!

Here are some more hot ideas from the world of advertising.

1 Smart
1 Tag
1 Euro

Rent a car/bike

People in two German cities, Berlin and Hamburg, can rent cars for only about US$1 a day! In addition, they don't pay anything extra if they drive a lot of kilometres.
So what's the deal? Well, ...
✘ You must rent the car for a minimum of three days.
✘ You must drive a minimum of 30 kilometres a day.

And the car?
✘ It's very, very small (a **Smart**).
✘ Its maximum speed is only 60 kilometres an hour.

But, ... The car is covered with ads!
The 'car rental' company is really an ad agency. It is making lots of money!
Their next idea: a rent-an-ad bike.

The idea is growing! You can now find this advertising idea in other German cities. And the Austrian racing driver, Niki Lauda, has started the same kind of cheap car-hire in Vienna. He hopes to expand to Spain and the Netherlands soon. Where next?

WORD FILE	
deal	A business agreement.
exploit (v)	To make money out of other people.
innovation	A product with new ideas.
🇺🇸 kilometer	🇬🇧 kilometre

Is the company exploiting people who just want to rent a car or bike? What do you think? Have you seen any other new ways of advertising? Can you think of any innovative ideas?

CONSUMER SPY

9

CHARITY SHOPS

It's great to buy new clothes... but what do you do with the old ones? Or what about the books that you won't read again? And your old CDs?

In a consumer society, we often have things that we don't use anymore.

But these things can be ideal for somebody else. One person's rubbish is often another person's treasure! But how can you find that person?

The shops

It's easy in the U.K. In every High Street, there are shops that sell these 'unwanted' objects.

These shops belong to different charity organisations. People bring their things here, and the shop sells them. The money goes to the charity.

There are a few rules:
- clothes must be washed and ironed;
- everything must be in good condition;
- electrical objects must be in working order.

The staff

Very often the people who work in the charity shops are volunteers. They don't get a salary. Some of them do it because they want to support the charity. Others do it for work experience. A lot of students have part-time jobs in these shops. They don't get any money, but they can learn a lot about customer relations, about display techniques, and about the charity itself. Sometimes, after they have finished their studies, they work for the charity as full-time employees.

In a modern society, the work that charities do is very valuable. There are so many people in every country who do not have enough food, or clothes, or a job. So any money that the 'rich' section of society can give to the poor section is important.

Where does your money go?

Some of the charities are very big organisations. They have a lot of staff, and big offices, and run sophisticated (and expensive) advertising campaigns. So there is a big question:

"How much money goes to the people who need it?"

Some charities keep 20% for their own expenses; some keep more. So ask a few questions before you give them money. Choose your charity carefully!

WORD FILE

charity	An organisation that helps poor or ill people.
customer relations	Communicating with customers to keep them happy.
display techniques	How to exhibit products well.
employee	A person who works for money.
part-time job	A job for only a few hours a day or week.
staff	The people who work for an organisation.
unwanted	The things people do not want to keep.
work experience	Learning about the world of work.
working order	When a machine can function.

🇺🇸 garbage   🇬🇧 rubbish

CONSUMER SPY: What charities do you know? What are their objectives? How do they collect money? Do they have other activities (e.g. shops)?

THE TRAVELS OF A BLOUSE

Some of the clothes which people give to charity travel a long way! Here is the 'travel diary' of a blouse. It travelled over 16,000 kilometres!

Early October 2003

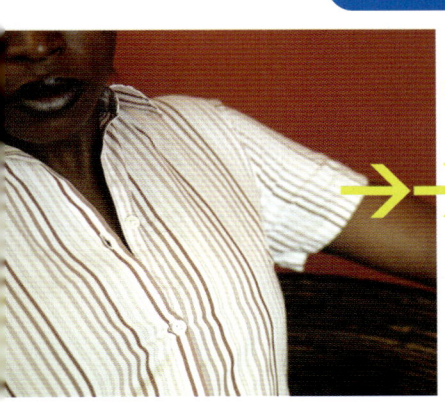

Dana Simons, a charity worker in a town in south-east England is clearing out her wardrobe. She finds a blouse at the back of it. It was expensive, but she's never worn it. She decides to take it to the recycling bank outside her local supermarket.

This bank belongs to the charity Scope, which provides money for people with cerebral palsy. Later that week, a recycling company collects all the clothes in the bank. This company pays money to Scope: in exchange, it can sell the clothes. The blouse travels 16 kilometres to the headquarters in Leicester. The people in the company check all the clothes carefully. They decide where to send them. They are sure that this blouse will be good in Africa. The material is light and cool. Also, it is top quality, so it is good for export. A worker packs the blouse with a lot of other clothes. Then some colleagues put the 45-kilo package into a container. A lorry takes this to a ship in Southampton, in the south of England. The container goes onto a ship, and the blouse's sea-journey begins.

November 2003

The ship, the St. Michigan, has gone south, through the Atlantic Ocean, into the Mediterranean Sea, and through the Suez Canal. Finally, it enters the Indian Ocean. After seven weeks, it arrives at the port of Beira, in Mozambique. The container with the blouse waits in Customs for a week. A huge lorry leaves the port with the container. It travels to the capital of Mozambique, Tete. The lorry crosses the wide Zambezi River and travels north with a police guard (the value of the contents is about $US 55,000). It enters Zambia and travels to the town of Chipata. This is the fourth biggest city in Zambia.

December 2003

A trader, Khalid, has bought the container of clothes. Three staff in his shop open it, and take out the 45-kilo package. He can sell it for about $US 300.
A market trader called Mary buys it. It contains hundreds of blouses, skirts, and other clothes. She opens it, and the blouse comes out. It looks good. It's top quality, and the colours are bright. She puts it on her market stall.

A teacher, Priscilla Msimuko, sees the blouse. She pays just under US$3 for it. That's more than a day's salary, but she feels pleased. "It's nice. I'll wear it to parties. It's important to look good."

Back in England, Dana is happy to hear that her blouse is making someone happy, and didn't end up on a rubbish dump.

WORD FILE

cerebral palsy	A disease that damages the brain.
clear out (v)	To throw away the things that you don't want.
container	A big metal or wood box that can go onto different lorries and ships.
Customs	The place where goods that enter a country are checked.
headquarters	The main office of an organization.
recycling bank	A container where people can put objects that can be recycled.
trader	A person who buys and sells things.

🇺🇸 color	🇬🇧 colour
garbage dump	rubbish tip
kilometer	kilometre
truck	lorry

Do you have any clothes that could be recycled in this way? Are there any organisations that can arrange this?

CONSUMER SPY

11

UNICEF WORKS!

What does UNICEF mean? United Nations Children's Fund.

What is it? An international organisation to protect children's rights through health care and education.

Where does it operate? In more than 160 countries. Its main office is in New York.

How does it operate? It works with governments on programmes for children.

Does it only work with children? It also works in communities to provide clean water, and on HIV-Aids programmes.

UNICEF has very many different projects, because countries and people's needs are different. It's not always so easy to make things change. You have to go step by step. It's not enough to give money. You can solve one part of the problem, but then another part of it appears!

Here is an example of a project in one country (Brazil). But the problem-solving approach is typical of UNICEF's work in other places, too.

WORD FILE

cardboard	Thick paper used for boxes.
garbage	The things which you throw away.
garbage dump	A place in or near a city for rubbish.
grab (v)	To take something quickly.
income	The money people get from their work.
integrate (v)	To become part of something.
middleman	A person who arranges business between other people.
rescue (v)	To save a person from danger.
self-confidence	Feeling good about your abilities.
shocking	Very surprising.
trash	Rubbish.
unemployed	With no job.

🇺🇸	🇬🇧
center	centre
garbage	rubbish
kids	children
truck	lorry

UNICEF in Brazil

There is a very important **UNICEF** project in the Brazilian city of Olinda. This began in 1992.

A big city problem
In many big cities today, there are a lot of unemployed people. Some of these families live in rubbish dumps. They make 'houses' out of pieces of cardboard and plastic. This sounds shocking... but in fact there are people sleeping in shop doorways and cardboard boxes in big cities like New York and London. They are mostly adults, but in this project, **UNICEF** wanted to rescue the children.

A family problem
In Olinda, some families lived in the rubbish dumps – but they also worked in them. The kids collected and recycled the rubbish, so they made money from the dumps. Their families needed this cash to survive. So – just taking the kids away from the rubbish dumps was not a good solution.

About 350 kids and teens lived and worked on the rubbish dump. When the rubbish truck arrived, they rushed to grab the rubbish. This was really dangerous. Some kids lost their arms and legs in the machines.

Finding a solution
UNICEF wanted to provide schools for the kids, but they understood that they had to compensate the parents for the loss of income. After all, some teenagers were earning around US$5 a day... and even the small kids could earn one dollar.

A practical approach
UNICEF helped the adult rubbish collectors to form an association. They could sell direct to the paper, glass and plastic industries, not to the 'middlemen'. As a result, they got more cash. Some families earned double their old incomes. So the money from the kids was not so important.

What about the kids and teenagers?
In 1998, a group of teenagers helped to renovate a building. It's now a youth centre. There are spaces for kids to come for pre-school and after-school activities. They can get help with their homework. They can have lessons in art and dance and music. They can recycle some of the rubbish to make objects to sell. To encourage education, **UNICEF** gives US$8 a month to every family whose kids attend school.

More problems
This was a very good solution to a big problem. The families got more money. The kids and teenagers went to school. Of course, that caused problems, too. Many of the teenagers from the rubbish dumps did not have any self-confidence. It was their first time in school. Some of them were 14 years old – but many of their classmates were only 7! It was difficult for all of them. And difficult for the teachers, too!

In fact, there was another **UNICEF** project to help these groups to integrate, and to provide extra help for the teachers. Slowly, the problems began to disappear.

Learning from experience: problem solving
The people involved in this project learned a lot. To make a successful project:

- families and communities must participate;
- the government (local, state and federal) must give support;
- extra support from private companies and workers' unions is also important.

There are now similar projects in ten other cities in Brazil. In the year 2004, approximately 1,500 of these kids from the rubbish dumps went to school. But there are 43,000 more who don't go. Brazil is a big country!

Do you know of any other projects to help children in your city or region? Can you buy T-shirts, or Christmas cards, or 'consume' other things to help?

Phones can do ANYTHING!

From here...

...To here.

Do you think that when Alexander Graham Bell invented the telephone at the end of the 19th century, he had any idea that it would become so important in the 21st century?

For over a hundred years, people used telephones just to talk to other people. You had to dial a number, and then wait for the operator to connect you. It was slow, but it was a great revolution. Until then, people in different places communicated mainly through the written word. But long-distance calls were expensive, and slow.

Towards the end of the 20th century, automatic connections became possible. Calls became quicker and cheaper. Calling a friend for a chat, even in a distant town, became more common. But you still needed to find a phone to call from.

Then suddenly, computer technology began to be used for phones. They became mobile. They became smaller and lighter. Lots of people carried them, and used them in the street, on buses and in public places – almost everywhere.

These phones could do lots of different things. Today, mobile phones can send text messages. Many of them have screens with colour. Some of them have little video cameras. Some phones can connect you to the Internet. You can receive and send e-mails, and download music. There is a new phone-feature every few months!

Mobile phones are now a 'must have' fashion item. Colour, design and materials are all really important. The models change every year.

They are also a favourite object for thieves, of course!

What are the most important features of a phone for you? What is your ideal phone?

CONSUMER SPY

WORD FILE	
connection	When one phone connects with another.
fashion item	An object that is bought to be in fashion.
mobile	Something you can move or carry.
operator	The person who used to connect phone speakers.
thief	A person who steals objects.

🇺🇸	🇬🇧
cellphone	mobile
center	centre
color	colour
favorite	favourite
kids	children

THE STATE OF OUR PLANET

THE WORLD
A lot of people think that our planet's in a bad state. We don't look after it. Here are three examples of environmental problems in many countries:

1 There are too many cars in city centres. They pollute the atmosphere. It's not even efficient to use a car: there are big traffic jams, and it's often impossible to find a parking place.

2 We produce more and more rubbish. There are huge rubbish dumps in most cities. Astronauts can even see a dump in New York City from space! A lot of the rubbish is plastic, and it survives for years and years.

3 Factory chimneys pollute the air. This affects birds, animals and humans. We all need to breathe clean air.

These are 'big' environmental issues. Many governments and city authorities have projects to make things better. But what can *you* do? What do *you* have control over? How can *you* make a difference?

AN ENVIRONMENTAL PROJECT
There's a great environmental project on the Internet. It's called **The Four Rs Project.** You solve three puzzle-questions and then discover a code word for a fourth area of action. Let's take a look.

MAKING A DIFFERENCE
What can we do about rubbish? The project suggests three 'R' ideas – and you discover a fourth one when you complete all four parts. (See pages 16 and 17.)

Here are the first three ideas:
REDUCE the amount of rubbish we make.
REUSE things: don't throw them away.
RECYCLE things: find other uses for things. Be inventive!

WORD FILE
environment	The air and earth around us.
look after (v)	To take care of a person or thing.
pollution	Things which make air, water or the earth dirty.
recycle (v)	To use an object in a different way.
reduce (v)	To make something smaller.
reuse (v)	To use an object again.
rubbish	The things that you throw away.
traffic jam	When the traffic cannot move.

🇺🇸 center / garbage   🇬🇧 centre / rubbish

CONSUMER SPY Look at the three examples of 'big' environmental problems. Are they a problem in your region? What other problems are there? Are there any projects to solve them?

AN ENVIRONMENTAL
>PROJECT

What's your advice?

There are four missions in the project. Select each mission in turn and choose the best environmental answers to some questions. Collect the three code words... and then discover the fourth code word after Mission 4. There are also some eco-friendly projects that you can do at home or at school.

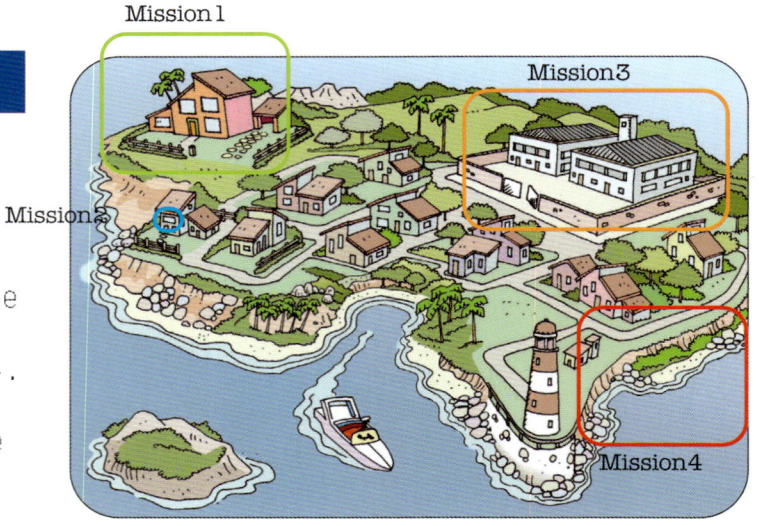

Mission 1
Mission 2
Mission 3
Mission 4

Mission 1:	Mission 2:	Mission 3:	Mission 4:
house	room	school	beach

REDUCE

Look at these rooms in the house and choose the best environmental advice for the people.

Ron's room

Computer
a) Leave it on all the time.
b) Turn it off when you're not using it.

T.V.
a) Turn it off if you're not watching a programme.
b) Keep it turned on, with the sound down.

Radio
a) Use normal batteries.
b) Use rechargeable batteries.

Kitchen

Taps
a) Turn them off firmly.
b) Let them drip.

Kettle
a) Fill it with water.
b) Put just enough water in it.

Washing machine:
a) Wait until there are enough clothes to fill it.
b) Wash a few clothes at a time.

Garage

Light
a) Leave it on.
b) Turn it off when you leave.

Car
a) Use it all the time.
b) Walk, or use a bike, for short trips.

Mission 1

CONSUMER SPY What can you reduce in your home? Make a list.

16

REUSE

Look at Mandy's room. It's a mess! Choose the best environmental advice to give her.

Comics and magazines	a) Leave them on the floor.
	b) Swap them with a friend.
Old clothes	a) Give them to your younger sister.
	b) Throw them away.
Plastic box	a) Hide it in the cupboard.
	b) Use it as a plant pot.

How many things can she reuse? Make a list.

Mission 2

RECYCLE

Look at the schoolyard. There's a lot of rubbish. What must they throw away? What can the students recycle? Write 'TA' or 'R'.

☐ plastic bottle   ☐ sweet papers
☐ paper bag   ☐ glass bottle
☐ drinks can

Mission 3

WORD FILE

battery	An object that supplies electricity.
belong (v)	To be a possession of a person.
code word	A secret word.
driftwood	Wood that is on the beach.
kettle	A metal container to boil water to make tea.
mess	When a place is untidy or dirty.
mission	An important journey or project.
rechargeable	Batteries that you can use many times.
safe	Not dangerous.
swap (v)	To exchange things.

🇺🇸	🇬🇧
candy	sweet
closet	cupboard
faucet	tap
garbage	rubbish
program	programme

???

What about nature? Take a look at the beach. Let's clean it. What are the best clothes to wear? What belongs there? What is it safe to pick up? What is dangerous (wear gloves)? What can we recycle?

A ☐
B ☐

☐ broken glass bottle
☐ driftwood
☐ fishing net
☐ plastic bottle
☐ rubber tire
☐ shells
☐ starfish
☐ syringe

Mission 4

The environmental code

reduce → reuse → recycle → r _ _ _ _ _ _

Can you choose the 'R' word to use when we are protecting our world?

(Answers on page 24.)

CONSUMER SPY — What about *your* environment (home/your room/school and nature)? Choose one of these. What good examples of reducing, reusing and recycling can you think of?

17

CONSUMER HOT TOPICS:

Food intake versus energy output

Isn't it strange? A large percentage of the world's population can't get enough to eat. But in 'advanced' societies, there's a different health problem. Obesity. And this problem is spreading to lots of different countries.

Why is this happening? What does it mean? Let's look at some of the facts.

Modern life is fast. Everyone is rushing. Right? So there's not much time for meals. And 'fast food' is easy to find (if you have the cash).
Fast food is fashionable. Millions of dollars are spent on ads to promote fast food and snacks.

The message?
Fast food is modern! It's cool! It's fun!

The facts?
Most fast food contains a lot of calories. And if the consumers don't take a lot of exercise, those calories produce fat.

Exercise?
If you live in a big city, and travel by car or bus, you probably don't take much daily exercise. This is worse if you sit at your computer, or watch videos, in your spare time.

It takes a lot of regular exercise to balance the effects of this kind of food. Let's look at four popular fast food products. How many calories do they contain?

Cola 500ml	= 210 Kcal
Burger and chips	= 699 Kcal
Banana milk shake	= 396 Kcal
Chocolate bar (large)	= 445 Kcal

CONSUMER SPY — What fast food and snacks have you eaten in the last 24 hours? What exercise have you taken in the same period?

OBESITY

Getting rid of the CALORIES

Here's what you have to do to 'negate' the effects of that food, and burn up those extra calories.

Cola:	More than 30 minutes' jogging.
Burger and chips:	Play football for more than one hour + jog for 43 minutes.
Milk shake:	One hour's cycling.
Chocolate bar:	Play football for more than one hour.

Surprised? Are there enough hours in the day to do these activities? Or is it easier to cut the calories?

ACTIVITY CHART

Let's look at this problem in a different way. You have 60 minutes to take some exercise.
What is the best activity to do? How many calories do different activities burn up in 60 minutes?

AEROBIC DANCING	390
CYCLING	372
DANCING	270
JOGGING	390
PLAYING FOOTBALL	420
PLAYING TENNIS	432
RUNNING UPHILL	582
WALKING	210

So... the choice is yours!

WORD FILE

balance (v)	An equal amount of two different things.
burn up (v)	To consume something.
calorie	A unit to measure energy from food.
fashionable	In fashion.
get rid of (v)	To dispose of something.
input	The things that go into something.
negate	To make something have no effect.
output	The things that go out of something.
rush (v)	To move very quickly.
spare time	Free time or leisure.
spread (v)	To extend the occurrence or influence.
uphill	To go up a hill or stairs.

🇺🇸 fries	🇬🇧 chips
soccer	football

Make a note of your calorie input for two days and your energy output. Is the balance 'positive' (more exercise than calories) or 'negative' (more calories than exercise)?

CONSUMER SPY

These statistics relate to young people in Britain. What about your country? Would any of them be similar? In our global world, a lot of problems are international. Perhaps some of the solutions are, too.

HEALTHY LIVING

Modern life: facts and figures

Visits to the doctor: 75-90% are stress-related.

Money spent by people aged between 8 and 16 on snacks on the way to and from school: Over US$ 500 million.

Percentage of young smokers who will die early: 25%

Important factors for a healthy life

We can consider several aspects of modern lives:

• **exercise**

Lack of exercise can lead to obesity, high blood pressure and heart disease. Many people use cars too much: walking and cycling are good for you!

• **diet**

We need a balanced diet, with food from all the main groups. Different people have different ideas about the percentages from each group. **Here's one suggestion**; do you agree with it?

One problem in a modern society is that we may eat a lot of processed foods. These often contain a lot of sugar and chemicals. These kinds of foods are one cause of obesity. Natural and organic foods may help us to avoid this.

• **emotional health**

Self image is very important, and is often a problem for teenagers. Diseases such as bulimia and anorexia are serious problems: don't neglect them! See the tips on the opposite page for some ideas.

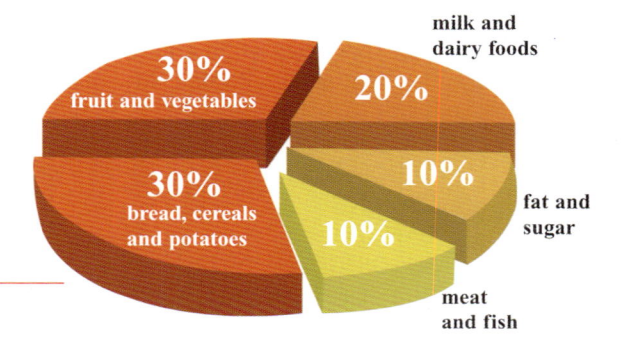

- 30% fruit and vegetables
- 20% milk and dairy foods
- 30% bread, cereals and potatoes
- 10% fat and sugar
- 10% meat and fish

Stress and depression can also affect our health. Don't let them affect you! Again, look at the tips opposite.

Helping ourselves

There are some ideas for Healthy Living on the Projects page. Take a look at them and see if they are good for you.

WORD FILE

anorexia	An illness where people become very thin.
bulimia	An illness where people vomit after eating.
cycling	Riding a bike.
depression	Feeling very unhappy.
disease	An illness.
lack	Without something.
neglect (v)	To not look after something.
obesity	Being overweight.
organic food	Food produced with no chemicals.
processed food	Food made by machines.
self-image	How you think of yourself.
tip	A good suggestion.

CONSUMER SPY — What are the things that affect health for you and your friends? Where can you find help?

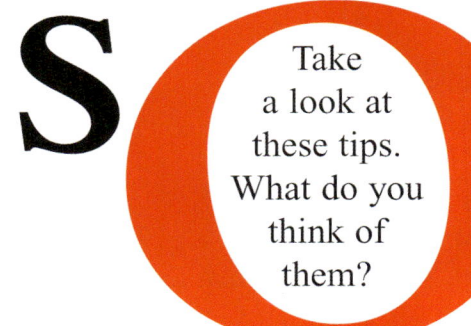

PROBLEM SOLVING

Take a look at these tips. What do you think of them?

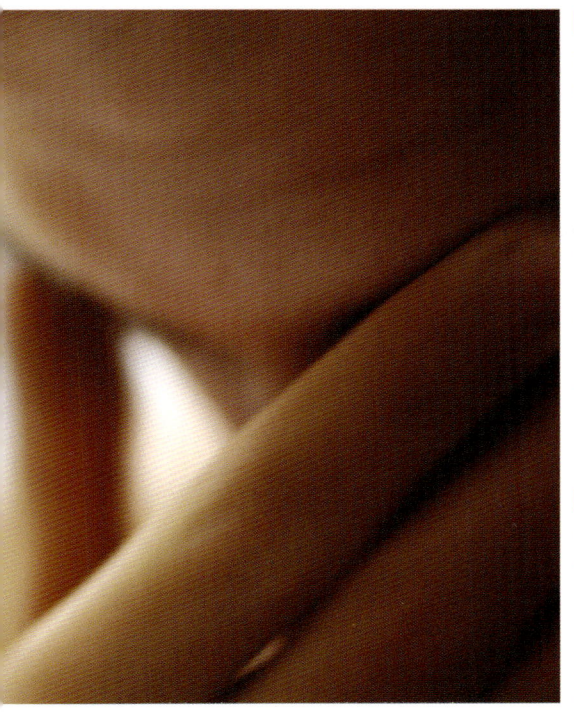

EATING DISORDERS

If you, or one of your friends, has an eating disorder, here are some things to remember.

* People with eating disorders often use food as a way of showing that they are unhappy.
* Being thin doesn't mean they have an eating disorder. There are other signs to look for.
* If you're worried about a friend, try to encourage them to get help.
* Never change your own eating patterns to fit in with theirs.
* If someone has an eating disorder, the first step to recovery is to admit it.
* This takes courage.
* Eating disorders can affect everyone.

DEPRESSION

Here are a few ways to feel happier.

* Do something you enjoy: watch a film you love, or listen to your favourite music.
* Get physical! Doing exercise usually makes you feel good about yourself.
* Share your problem. Discussing it with a friend often helps.
* Remember that sad feelings will go away. Nothing lasts forever.
* Don't hesitate to talk to sympathetic teachers and parents.
* See a health professional. Remember that they will respect your privacy.

CONSUMER SPY — Make your own list of tips for some Healthy Living problems.

STRESS

Sometimes, life seems full of problems.

* It's normal to be nervous before exams!
* Headaches, stomach pains, sleeping problems and no interest in food can all be signs of stress. Be alert!
* Write a list of the things that make you feel stressed. Think of a solution for each one.
* Make an action plan, and discuss this with a friend.
* Eating properly can reduce stress. Every day, try to eat five portions of fruit and vegetables and to drink eight glasses of water.
* Laughing is a great way to reduce stress! People say that 100 laughs are as good as 15 minutes on your bike!

WORD FILE

action plan	A list of things to do.
admit (v)	To say a thing is true.
eating disorder	An illness connected with food.
eating pattern	The kind of food you eat every day.
fit in (v)	To be the same as, or part of something.
health professional	A doctor, nurse, or health worker.
hesitate (v)	To wait before doing something.
recovery	Getting better from an illness.
reduce (v)	To get smaller.
share (v)	To divide something with another person.
solution	The answer to a problem.

🇺🇸 favorite movie   🇬🇧 favourite film

Consumers quiz
Do you know?

(Answers on page 24.)

1. CHOCOLATE FACTS

What do we call these things? Match the words to find out.

- [ ] BAKED ALASKA
- [ ] CAPPUCCINO
- [ ] CHOCAHOLIC
- [ ] CHOCOLATE CHIP COOKIES
- [ ] CHOCOLATE MILK SHAKE
- [ ] COCOA
- [ ] MEXICO
- [ ] TIRAMISU

a   A person who really loves chocolate.
b   An ice-cream pudding with hot chocolate sauce.
c   North American cookies with small pieces of chocolate.
d   A cold drink of chocolate and milk.
e   A white coffee with grated chocolate on top.
f   A North Italian pudding with chocolate, cream and cake. Its name means 'upside down'.
g   The plant that chocolate is made from.
h   Chocolate was taken to Europe in the 16th century from this country.

2. WATER INDUSTRY

How many litres of water are necessary to manufacture these things?

a   1 liter of beer
   i under 10 litres   ii 10-15 litres   iii over 15 litres
b   A newspaper
   i 1 litre   ii 5 litres   iii 10 litres
c   A cotton shirt
   i 50 litres   ii 100 litres   iii 150 litres
d   A car tyre
   i 10,000 litres   ii 20,000 litres   iii 30,000 litres

3. MONEY WORD PUZZLE

Find these kinds of money in the word puzzle. The first letters are supplied for you.

a   Some parents give (p ●●●) money to their children.
b   The extra money that people leave in a restaurant. (t ●●●)
c   The money you pay on a bus. (f ●●●)
d   Credit cards are (p ●●●) money.
e   People get this when they work. (s ●●●)
f   The money that you sometimes get back. (c ●●●)
g   The money that you are keeping for the future. (s ●●●)
h   If people lose a pet, they sometimes offer this money. (r ●●●)
i   The money which something costs. (p ●●●)
j   Metal money. (c ●●●)

```
S A V I N G S X Z
A F T B P R T Q V
L A X P O C K E T
A R Z L I D W B I
R E W A R D U F P
Y G S S A Y R T M
O C Z T C O I N S
M P R I C E F Q U
K T X C H A N G E
```

22

Projects

SHOPPING MALLS
Visit your favorite shopping mall. Count the stores. Put them in categories (clothes, music, shoes...). List the eating places. What types are there? What nationalities? What other things are there in the mall? What makes this mall different from others? What is positive? What is negative? Design an ad for it with all its positive features.

1

TRAFFIC SURVEYS: HOW MUCH TRAFFIC IS THERE?
Work in a group. Choose a specific road. Make a note of the traffic that passes you at different times of the day. Note the types of traffic (e.g. cars, bikes, lorries, buses). Do this on the same day for several weeks, or for different days in one week. Compare the results.

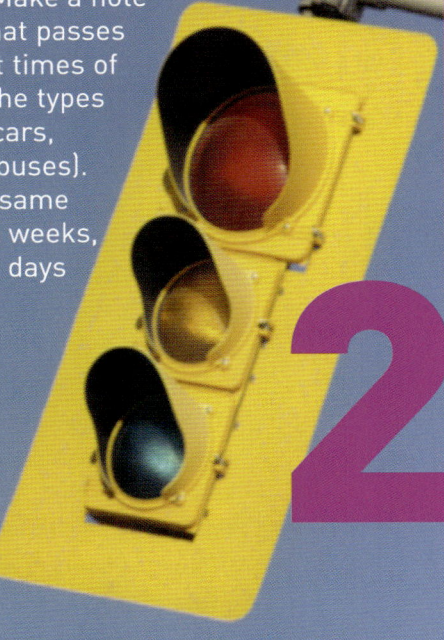

2

WHAT ABOUT WASTE?
Make a note of all the things your family throws away in 24 hours. Put it in categories, e.g. paper, plastic, aluminium. Can you think of ways to **R**educe, **R**euse or **R**ecycle any of this? Design a poster with your suggestions.

3

HEALTHY FOOD ADS
Look at the advertising aimed at young people for snacks or fast food in magazines, on TV and in posters. Analyse the techniques that they use, and decide which ones work well. Choose a healthy food to advertise. Decide the best way to do this. What will you emphasise? How can you attract people's attention? Design your ad.

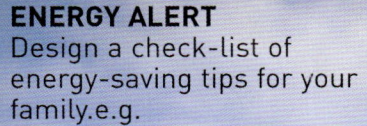

4

ENERGY ALERT
Design a check-list of energy-saving tips for your family. e.g.
- Switch off lights when not in use.
- Don't leave hot taps running.
- Don't leave TVs or computers on stand-by.

5

CONSUMER SONG CHART
Lots of songs are about money. Here are three. 'The money kept rolling in' (Madonna, in 'Evita'); 'Can't buy me love' (the Beatles); 'Money for nothing' (Dire Straits). There are also songs about ecology and the environment. Choose a topic and see how many songs you can find for it. Make a Top Ten Music Chart.

6

CONSUMER SPY Collect your favorite Consumer SPY mini-projects. Make an exhibition of them with your friends. Design a poster to advertise it and a guide to the exhibition. Invite other friends, your families and teachers.

Topics chatrooms

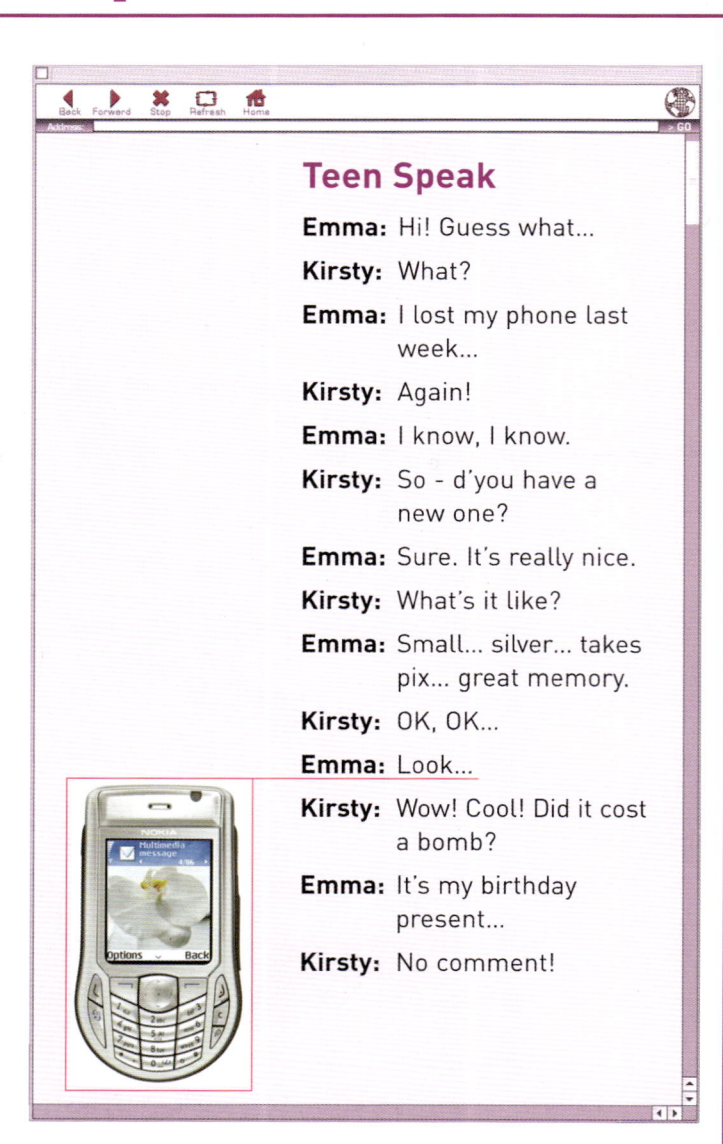

Teen Speak

Emma: Hi! Guess what...
Kirsty: What?
Emma: I lost my phone last week...
Kirsty: Again!
Emma: I know, I know.
Kirsty: So - d'you have a new one?
Emma: Sure. It's really nice.
Kirsty: What's it like?
Emma: Small... silver... takes pix... great memory.
Kirsty: OK, OK...
Emma: Look...
Kirsty: Wow! Cool! Did it cost a bomb?
Emma: It's my birthday present...
Kirsty: No comment!

Can you believe it?

William Wordsworth is one of the most famous English poets. He criticised many things in his 'modern' society. He thought that things connected with nature were better.

> *The world is too much with us: late and soon,*
> *Getting and spending, we lay waste our powers:*
> *Little we see in nature that is ours.*

He wrote this in 1806. Two hundred years ago, people used a lot of energy to make and to consume things. In fact, Britain was already a consumer society! How about your country?

Fun chat

Money Proverbs and Sayings

Money doesn't grow on trees.

Money makes the world go round.

All that glitters is not gold.

Love of money is the root of all evil.

Facts Check

Pages 16-17: MISSION 1: Ron's room: b/a/b; Kitchen: a/b/a; Garage: b/b. MISSION 2: b/a/b. MISSION 3: Throw away: sweet papers; Recycle: other things. MISSION 4: Best clothes: picture B; Belongs there: driftwood/shells/starfish; Safe to pick up (recycle): rubber tyre/fishing net/plastic bottle; Dangerous (wear gloves): broken glass bottle/syringe
Code Word 4: RESPECT

Page 22: CHOCOLATE: a Chocaholic; b Baked Alaska; c Chocolate chip cookies; d Chocolate milk shake; e Cappuccino; f Tiramisu; g Cocoa; h Mexico
WATER: a ii; b iii; c iii; d ii
MONEY: a Pocket; b Tip; c Fare; d Plastic; e Salary; f Change; g Savings; h Reward; i Price; j Coins

GOODBYE!

We're at the end of 'Consumers'. We hope that you'll continue with the Consumer Spy ideas. Be an intelligent consumer! See you in the next Topics title. Till then...

Susan Holden